Language Through Music
Book 3

An essential companion for early learning
and the teaching of English
as a foreign language

by Caroline and Ben Lumsden

school   days and dates   birthdays   party games   work and play   time and timetables

EDITION PETERS

London · Frankfurt · Leipzig · New York

For our namesakes Caroline and Ben Howarth

Peters Edition Limited
10–12 Baches Street
London
N1 6DN

Tel: 020 7553 4000
Fax: 020 7490 4921
e-mail: sales@uk.edition-peters.com
Internet: www.edition-peters.com

First published 2002
© 2002 by Hinrichsen Edition, Peters Edition Limited, London

ISBN 1 901507 97 1

A catalogue record for this book is available from the British Library

Music-setting by Andrew Jones

Cover and CD design and concept: www.adamhaystudio.com
Original artwork by Kate Hawley

Printed in Great Britain by Caligraving Limited
Thetford, Norfolk

Foreword

Language Through Music is a series of song books for teachers, group leaders, parents and grandparents. The books have been written specifically for those teaching students of English as a foreign language as well as children at foundation stage and key stages 1 and 2. In our household, the songs are sung and enjoyed by three-year-olds to ninety-three-year-olds!

Three books cover basic commands, actions, questions and answers through the following topics:

> Book 1: Names   Actions   Numbers   The Alphabet   Objects   Colour   Pets and Farm Animals
> Book 2: Family and Home   Face and Body   Monsters   Clothes   Food   Zoo Animals
> Book 3: School   Days and Dates   Birthday   Party Games   Work and Play   Time and Timetables

All the songs can be sung without accompaniment and can be learnt easily by playing copycat. Children do enjoy live accompaniments, however, so simple piano parts and guitar chords are provided for those lucky enough to have players to hand. The companion CD's provide further options, both for learning the songs and for lively backing in performance.

We have included as many ideas and suggestions as possible to create a compact and portable reference library. All the songs and actions should be used to stimulate ideas from the children and for creative activities. Around the edges of the text pages are suggestions of words or actions that you can make into flash cards as extra resource material.

All the related activities for each song have been graded with a star system:

> *easily managed   **moderately difficult   ***more difficult.

This is useful if you want to reinforce a particular teaching point by returning to a familiar song with a new, more difficult game, or to adapt the different levels for different age groups.

We would like to record our gratitude to all the children who have worked on the songs with us in France and England. In France, thanks go to Madame Fontaine and the children of École Jean Bouchet, Beaugeay and Marie Christine and the children of École Champlain, Brouage, Charente Maritime; in England, Glyn Oxley, Rebecca Peacock, Kirsten Schofield, Heather Graham and Janet Kerr, and the children of Beauchamp Music Group, Churcham, Gloucestershire. Special thanks go to William, Christopher, Bethan, Sophie, Madeline, Friederike, Rosie, Rosemary, Heather, Sophie, Georgina and Annabelle for their contribution to the CD, and to Kirsten Graham of Horfield Primary School, Westbury on Trym, Bristol, who acted as consultant and provided percussion ideas for the project.

Caroline and Ben Lumsden

Guitar chords to accompany the songs

Major chords

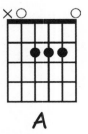
A

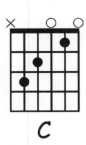
C

D

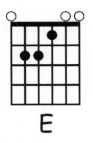
E

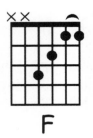
F

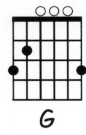
G

Seventh chords

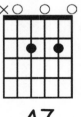
A7

B7

C7

D7

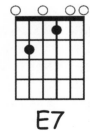
E7

G7

Minor chords

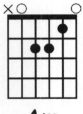
Am

Bm

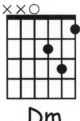
Dm

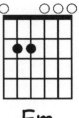
Em

Fm

Minor seventh chord

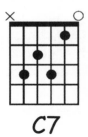
Am7

Contents

Good morning, class

1-4

2. Leader: Good morning, Fred.
   Fred: Good morning, Mister English teacher.
   Leader: How are you, Fred?
   Fred: I'm fine thanks, Mister English teacher.

How are you?

Doctor

Master

Miss

Madam

Sir

Mister

*Click and sing
Sing *Good morning, class.*
The group replies. Everyone
clicks rhythmically, putting
two clicks before the leader
sings, and four before
the reply.

*Good morning class
Leader: *"Good morning, class."*
Reply: *"Good morning,
Mr/Mrs/Miss English teacher."*
Leader: *"How are you, class?"*
Reply: *"We're fine thanks,
Mr/Mrs/Miss English teacher."*

*Use a puppet
Use a puppet as
the 'English teacher',
to say or sing
"Good morning, class."

*How are you, Bruce?
Leader: *"Good morning, Bruce."*
Reply: *"Good morning,
Mr/Mrs/Miss English teacher."*
Leader: *"How are you, Bruce?"*
Reply: *"I'm fine thanks,
Mr/Mrs/Miss English teacher."*
Change over.

**Good afternoon/ evening
Sing *"Good afternoon"* or
"good evening, class."
The group replies,
adding the clicks
as *Click and sing.*

**Change leaders
Ask someone else to be
the English teacher to say
or sing *Good morning, class.*

***Puppet conversation
Work in pairs, using a puppet or
cuddly toy to make conversation.
Puppet: *"Good morning,
          (Charlotte)."*
Voice 2: *"Good morning,
          (Zacky)."*
Puppet: *"How are you
          (Charlotte)?"*
Voice 2: *"I'm fine, thanks.
          How are you?"*
Puppet: *"Very well, thank
          you."*
Change over.

***Other greetings
Discuss other ways
of greeting people.
There are some
ideas around the page.
How do you greet
your friends?

What is this?

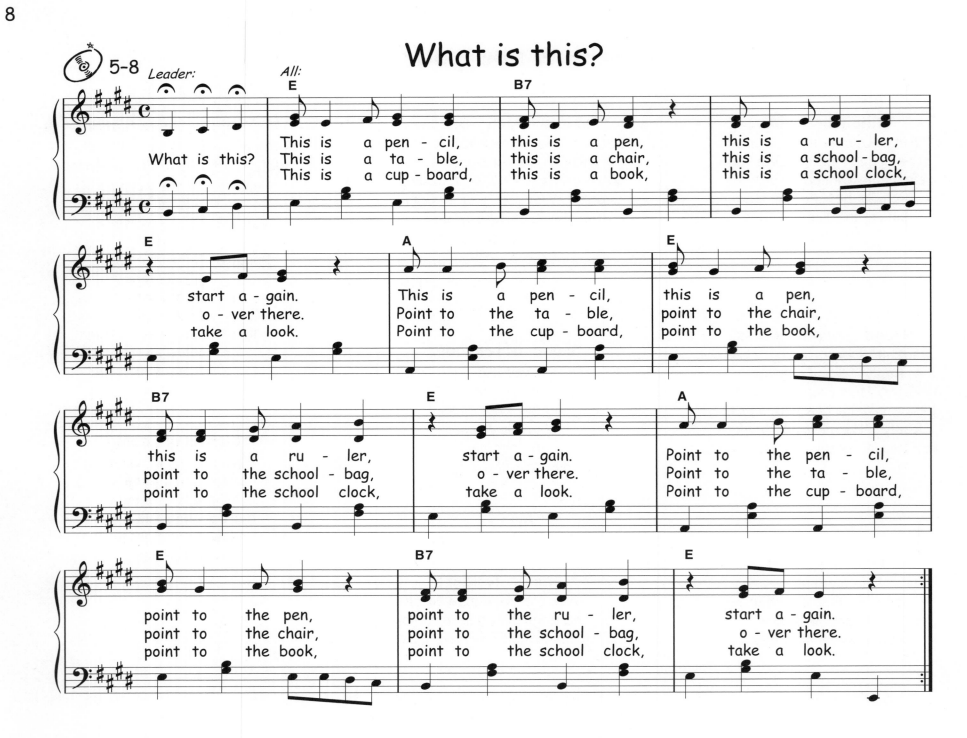

Is this a rubber.

No, it's a rubber.

Is this a book?

No, it's a pen

Is this a table?

Is this a pen?

No, it's a chair.

Is this a pencil?

No, it's a book.

This is a ...

*Sing and show
Sing verse one of
What is this? holding
up a pencil, pen and ruler.
Everyone joins in, holding
up the same items from
their own pencil cases.

*Point and sing
Sing verse 2 and
point to the three
items. Everyone
joins in pointing
and singing.

*Do the same
Do the same for
verse 3.

*Point to a pen
Write the names
of the items in the song
on the board, and everyone
has either to hold up or
point at whatever item
the leader points to.

**What is this?
Hold up an item and
say *"What is this?"*
Take it in turns to reply.

**Change items
As long as the words
'pen', 'chair' and 'book' are
kept for the rhyme, other
items can be put into the song.
There are some suggestions
at the bottom of
this page.

**Is this a pencil?
Hold up a book
and say, *"Is this a pencil?"*
Everyone replies,
"No, it is a book."

**Messages
In pairs, draw messages
to each other, e.g.
(John): *"Hello Amy, what is this?"*
(John has drawn a clock).
(Amy): *"Hello John, it is a clock.
What is this?"* (Amy draws a book)

***Memory bag
Pick up a pen from
your bag and say,
"In my bag I have a pen".
The next person says:
"In my bag I have a pen and
(holding up a pencil)
a pencil" and so on
until everyone has
added a word.

***Black magic
"Is it the pen?"
One person is told
the secret, i.e. that
the object chosen for
the game will be the one
after a black object has
been pointed to. He or she
goes outside the room while
the rest choose an object.
When the 'magician' returns
the leader asks,
"Is it the pencil?" "No."
"Is it the blackboard?" "No."
"Is it the pen?" "Yes!"

What day is it today?

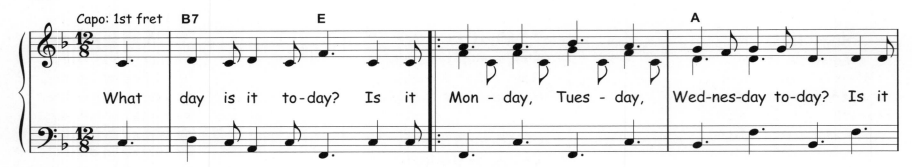

Leader: What day is it today?
          Is it Monday, Tuesday, Wednesday today?
          Is it Thursday, Friday or Saturday today or
          Sunday, Monday, Tuesday, Wednesday today?
          Is it Thursday, Friday–Saturday?

All: "Today is ..."

Is it Monday?

*Sing the question
Sing *What day is it today?* Everyone joins in and one person replies, *"Today is ..."* Repeat.

*Design your own
Make flash cards of the days of the week. Everyone can design their own.

*It is Monday
Hold up the flash cards, one at a time. Everyone chants *"It is Monday ..."* and so on.

**Change order
As *It is Monday* but change the order of the cards.

**Is it Monday?
Leader: *"Is it Monday?"*
Reply: *"No. It is Tuesday."*
Change leaders.

**Circle and sing
Choose someone to be in the middle of a circle. Everyone else joins hands and dances round, singing *What day is it today?* The person in the middle says, *"It is Monday."* He/she then rejoins the circle and sends another person to the middle for the next response, and so on.

**Chant the days
Chant the days of the week in order, Monday through to Sunday, all together or one after the other round the group.

***Find your partner
Use two sets of flash cards for the days of the week. Give each person a card, which they must not show anybody else. Then each person asks, one at a time, *"(Joe) have you got (Friday)?"* Go on until everyone finds their correct partner.

***What days do you go to school?/stay at home
"What days do you go to school?"
Reply: *"I go to school on ..."*
"What days do you stay at home?"
Reply: *"I stay at home on ..."*
Change leader.

***What is/was the day tomorrow/yesterday?
"What is the day tomorrow?"
Reply: *"Tomorrow is ..."*
"What was the day yesterday?"
Reply: *"Yesterday was ..."*
Change leader.

12

What's the date today?

*What's the date today?

Sing the first section of
What's the date today?
every time you meet your group.
Ask one person to write the
date on the board.

*Chant

Chant the names of the
months, tapping a rhythm
of two beats for each month.
The first syllable of July,
September, October,
November and December
come before the beat.

*Make flash cards

Make flash cards
for the months of
the year. Use these with
number cards to play
the date game .

***First, second, third

Teach 1st, 2nd, 3rd,
4th–31st.
Chant the numbers,
in order,
round the group.

**The date game

Using flash cards
of the months and number
cards, choose two people
to hold up the correct cards
as you sing the first section of
What's the date today?
e.g. *"January 5th"*,
"February 11th",
and so on.

***How many days?

Ask how many days
each month has, and
ask someone to
write on the board
e.g. January = 31

***Sing the date

One person is chosen
to say or sing the date
of his/her choice.

Happy birthday, Caroline

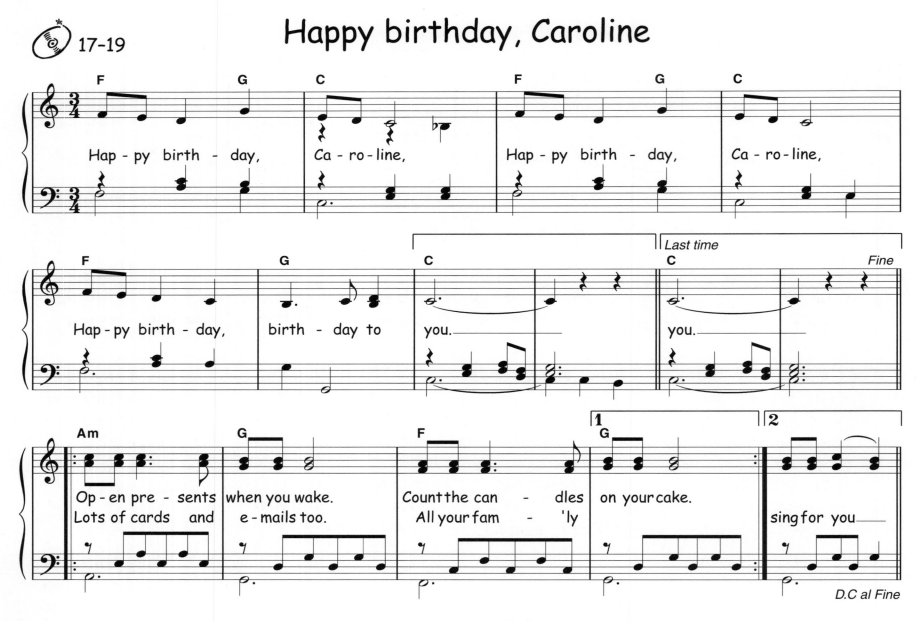

2. Now you're (eight) the time has come, for party games and lots of fun.
   All your friends, and granny too, will celebrate and sing for you ...

When is your birthday?

*Sing happy birthday ...
Sing *Happy birthday Caroline* changing the name and age for who-ever has a birthday.

*Hands up!
"Put your hands up if your birthday is in January", etc.

**Write and show
Everyone writes on a piece of card the month of his/her birthday. The leader asks all those with birthdays in March (for example) to hold up their cards.

**When is your birthday?
Leader: *"When is your birthday?"*
Reply: *"My birthday is in (March)."*
Change leaders.

**Card game
Everyone holds up their date cards so that the leader can ask,*"(Nicholas), when is (Sadie's) birthday."*
Reply: *"It is in (March)."*

**Write and sing
Everyone writes down the date of their birthday. Six people are chosen to stand at the front holding up what they have written. Sing *Whats the date today* using these dates for the song.

***Birthday conversation
Voice 1: *"Good morning (John)."*
Voice 2: *"Good morning (Tom)."*
Voice 1: *"How old are you?"*
Voice 2: *"Nine. How old are you?"*
Voice 1: *"Ten. When is your birthday?"*
Voice 2: *"February 16th. When is yours?"*
Voice 1: *"March 20th. You are older than me."*

***Stand in line
Ask the group to put them-selves in a long line with the oldest member of the group at the front.
Leader: *"Stand up if you have a birthday in January. (Sadie) when is your birthday?"*
Sadie: *"January 21st."*
Leader: *"(Jake) when is your birthday?"*
Jake: *"January 5th."*
Leader: *"Jake, you go to the front, and Sadie you go next."*
And so on.

Have a happy, hippy, hoppy, happy birthday

20-24

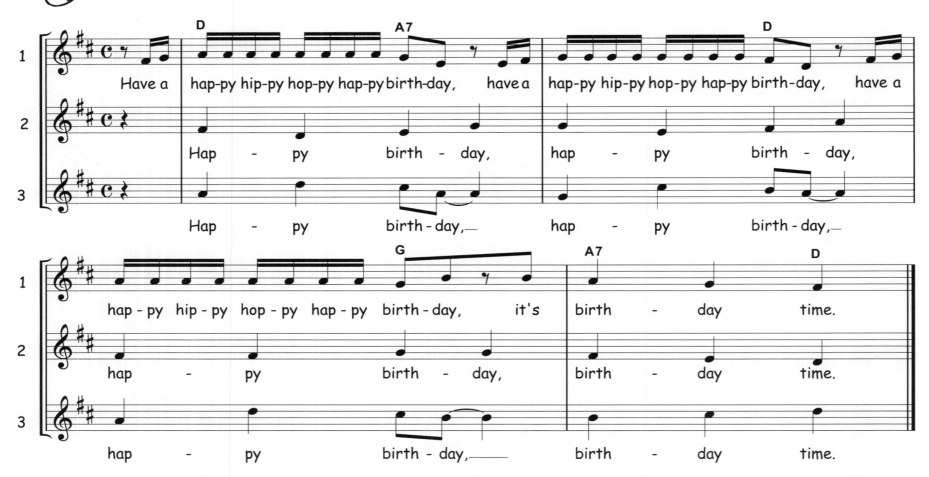

*Sing line 1
Learn the first
line of this three-
part round, before
trying the other lines.

**2 parts
When everyone is
really comfortable singing
"Have a happy, hippy ..."
learn line two and
divide into two groups.

***3 parts
When parts one
and two are secure,
learn line three, before
singing the whole
song as a round.

Party time

*Stand up if ...

Choose a leader to say
*"Stand up if you have
three sisters."*
*"Stand up if you have
blue eyes."*
*"Stand up if you are
wearing jeans."* etc

*Chocolate game

Collect a plate,
an unwrapped bar of
chocolate, a knife and fork,
a large dice, a hat, coat,
scarf and gloves. Everyone
sits in a circle while the dice
is passed round and thrown
by each person in turn. The
first person to throw a 6
runs to the middle of the
circle, puts on the items of
clothing and proceeds to cut
a piece of chocolate and eat
it, until the next person to
throw a 6 takes all the items
from him and starts
to put them on.

**Name game

Put out an alphabetical
list of names and places
jumbled up. Start
the game by saying:
"Anita went to America."
The next person continues:
"Barry went to Brazil."
and so on.

**Place the card

For this game you need a
music player and plenty of space.
The leader gives out playing cards to
half the group who form a circle.
The rest of the group form an outer
circle round them. The inner group
walks one way when the music starts
and the outer group the other way.
When the music stops the leader
says *"elbow to leg"* and each person
from the inner circle places the card
between their elbow and the leg of
the person opposite in the outer
circle. The last couple to do it are
'out.' And so it continues with
different parts of the body until
a winning couple is left.

***Elephant game

When you know lots
of animal names play
An elephant never forgets.
Take it in turns to name an
animal starting with each
letter of the alphabet.
If someone can't think
of one, they place their
hands on their head and
the game passes to
the next person.

***Riddles

Use some of the items
mentioned in the *Alphabet
song* in Book 1 as riddles, e.g.:

*"I am brown
and hairy.
What am I?"*

*"I am yellow
and furry. What
am I?"*

or make up your own.

Cows go moo, diggery doo!

25-28

Capo: 3rd fret

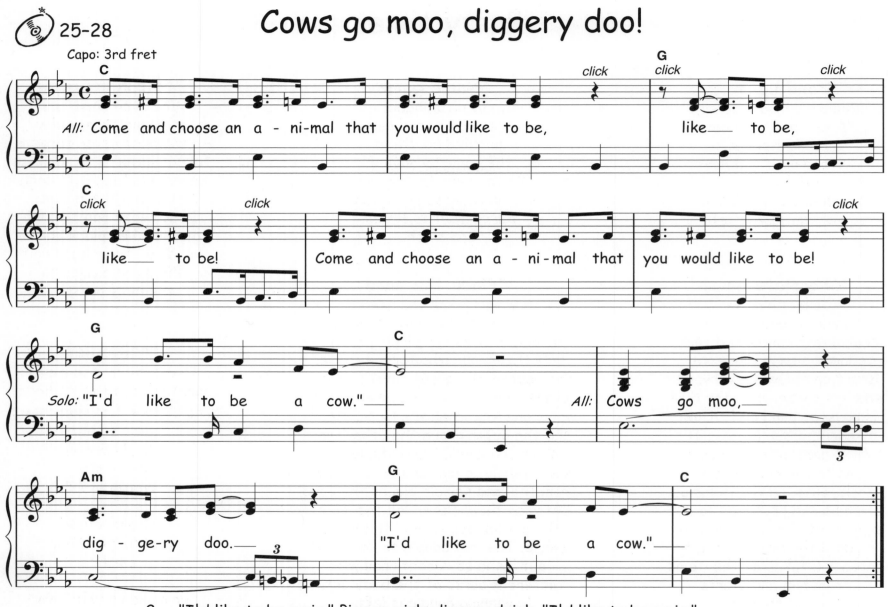

2. "I'd like to be a pig." Pigs go oink, diggery doink. "I'd like to be a pig."
3. "I'd like to be a hen." Hens go cluck, diggery duck. "I'd like to be a hen."
4. "I'd like to be a sheep." Sheep go baa, diggery daa. "I'd like to be a sheep."

Squeak, piggy, squeak

*Choose an animal
Four people are chosen
to be a cow, pig, hen and
sheep. Everyone sings
Cows go moo, diggery doo!
with the chosen four
singing the solo lines
"I'd like to be a ..."

*Spin the board
Everyone stands in a
circle singing *Cows go moo*.
The leader spins a wooden
cheese board in the middle
of the circle, then touches
someone on the shoulder who
has to run and catch the board
before it falls over. That
person then sings what
animal he would
like to be.

*I-spy
The leader says:
*"I spy with my little eye
something beginning with 'b'."*
(Sound the letter.)
Change over.

**Squeak, piggy, squeak
Choose someone to
go into the middle of
the circle. Blindfold him.
Spin him round, and walk
him towards someone.
When he touches that person
he says, *"Squeak, piggy, squeak"*
and when that person squeaks
he has to say, *"It is ..."*
If he answers correctly, that
person is blindfolded,
and so on.

**Pass the shoe
For this game everyone needs
to sit in a circle and take off
one of their shoes. Say,
" One, two, three: pass"
and everyone passes their
shoe to the person on the
right, and so on. When the
group is good at this,
try singing *Cows go moo*
as you pass the shoe.
(Use a teddy or football
for younger children.)

***Tail on the donkey
Draw a donkey (without a tail)
and put it on a pin board.
Everyone draws a tail.
One at a time each person is blindfolded and asked to pin their tail
onto the donkey. The person
who places their tail nearest to
the correct point on the
donkey wins the game.

***Make a snapdragon.
Make a snapdragon
(as in Book 1 page 31)
in order to play
"You are a fat, red donkey!"

***Pass the orange
Divide the group into
teams standing in a long line.
Give the front person an orange to
put under his chin. The orange is
then passed from person to person
without using hands until the end
of the line. The first team to finish
should sit down. If the orange is
dropped the team has
to start again.

Today, tomorrow, yesterday

To - day, to-mor - row, yes - ter-day, to - day we're going to draw. Please draw a fish, please

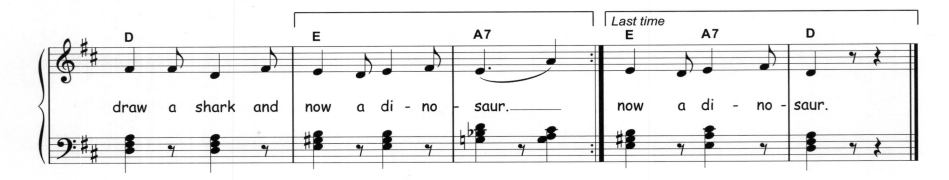

draw a shark and now a di - no - saur. now a di - no - saur.

Last time

2. Today, tomorrow, yesterday, today we're going to draw.
   Please draw a mouse, please draw a horse and now a dinosaur.

3. Today, tomorrow, yesterday, today we're going to draw.
   Please draw a pig, please draw a cow and now a dinosaur.

4. Today, tomorrow, yesterday, today we're going to draw.
   Please draw a frog, please draw a fox and now a dinosaur.

Big, bigger, biggest

*Sing and draw
Sing *Today, tomorrow, yesterday* while someone runs to the board to draw the animals (outline only) in the song.

*Draw a dinosaur
Divide into two teams. Each team sends someone to draw the animals in the song, while the leader is singing. A second person takes over for the second verse and so on.

*Add more
Add more verses to the song. There are some ideas around the page to help.

**Big and small
Make two lists, one for small animals and one for big ones. Take it in turns to say e.g. *"A lion is bigger than a penguin."*

**Memory game
Collect together a number of toy animals on a tray. Uncover the tray for ten seconds to allow the group to memorise the objects.

**Is it bigger than?
Cover the animals over again. Choose a new leader to ask *"Is the cow bigger than the horse?"* Reply: *"No, the horse is bigger."* *"Which is the smallest animal?"* Change leaders.

**Draw objects
Draw three objects on the board, e.g. a bird, a hat and a tree and ask questions such as: *"Is the tree smaller than the bird?"* Reply: *"No, the tree is bigger than the bird"* or *"Is the hat the biggest?"* Reply: *"The hat is not the biggest, the tree is."* And so on.

***Smaller/taller
Choose three people to stand in line and choose another person to be the leader. The leader asks the rest of the group, *"Is (Naomi) smaller than (John)?"* Reply: *"Yes, (Naomi) is smaller than (John)"* or *" No, (Naomi) is taller than (John)."* Leader: *"Who is the tallest, (Naomi, John or George)?"* Reply: *"(George) is the tallest."*

rat cat dinosaur
bat snake dinosaur
hare sheep dinosaur

goose bear dinosaur
duck moose dinosaur
hen goat dinosaur

What would you like to do today?

33-36

What would you like to do— to-day, do— to-day, do— to - day? Oh,

what would you like to do— to - day? "Go to the ci - ne-ma please!"_ (Oh)

2. Oh, what would you like to do today, do today, do today?
Oh, what would you like to do today? "Go to a football match please!"

3. Oh, what would you like to do today, do today, do today?
Oh, what would you like to do today? "Go to the swimming pool please!"

I'd like to fly an aeroplane

*Sing lines 1, 2 and 3
Learn each of the parts
separately before singing
all the way through this
three-part round.

**Sing 2 parts
Divide into two groups.
Group 1 starts from the
beginning when group 2
reaches the second line.

***Sing 3 parts
Finally sing all three
parts as a round, finishing
when group 1 has sung
twice through.

pottery hockey

music netball

painting rugby

drama ten pin bowling

gymnastics fishing

reading chess

cricket cards

My favourite activities

*Sing and reply

Ask who likes football.
Divide the group in two,
those who like the game
and those who don't. Then
sing *Football is the best!*
One group sings *"Yes it is!"*
and the other group
"No it's not!"

*Change leaders

As above, but a new leader
sings verse 2. Those who
like cricket sing *"Yes it is!"* and
the others *"No it's not!"* Change
leaders for the other verses.

*Test the leader

Everyone writes the name
of their favourite sport on a piece
of paper and hides it behind their
back. The leader has to guess their
favourite. If he guesses correctly
he gains a point; if not, a point
is given to the group.

**List and tell

Everyone lists three of
their favourite activities.
Ask *"What are your
favourite activities?"*
Reply: *"I like ..., ... and ..."*
Leader: *"Which do you like best?"*
Reply: *"I like ... best."*

**Choose and sing

One person sings
... is the best choosing
an activity that they
like, e.g. swimming. There
are more ideas to help
around the page.

**Find or make

Find a picture book
of activities. If this is not
possible design your own by
asking each person to draw an
activity. Hold up the book and
say: *"What is (Johnny) doing?"*
Reply: *"(Johnny) is swimming"* or
"(Johnny) is cycling" etc.

***Conversation

Voice 1: *"Do you like (running)?"*
Voice 2: *"No, I prefer (cycling)!"*
"Do you like (cycling)?"
Voice 1: *"Yes I do, but I like to
(swim) and play tennis too."*
Voice 2: *"I like (swimming) too."*

***Picture game

Divide into two teams.
Give one person from
each team a card with
the name of an activity
on it. They must then
draw that activity for
their team to guess. The
person drawing cannot speak,
only nod 'Yes' or 'No'.
Continue until every-
one has had a go or
until a cut off time,
at which point the
team with the most
correct guesses
is the winner.

Football is the best

42-45

Capo: 3rd fret

2. Oh cricket is the best ...
3. Oh netball is the best ...
4. Oh rugby is the best ...
5. Oh hockey is the best ...
6. Oh tennis is the best ...
Last time: Oh football is the best ... Yes it is!

My mother drives a tractor

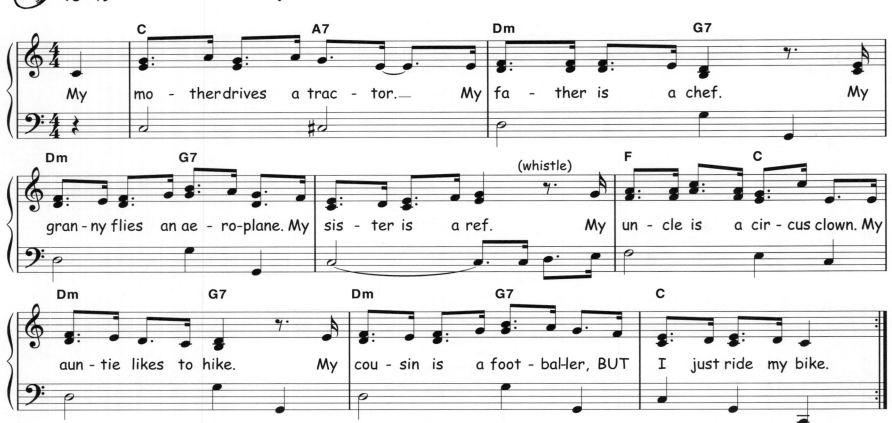

2. My mother feeds her chickens.
    My father cooks roast pork.
    My grandad likes to parachute.
    My granny likes to talk.
    My uncle likes to make us laugh;
    His jokes are all alike.
    My brother plays the violin,
    BUT I just ride my bike.

3. My mother counts her rabbits.
    My father bakes a pie.
    My granny likes to bungy jump.
    My grandad likes to fly.
    My auntie likes to roller blade.
    My uncle's name is Mike.
    My cousin is a movie star,
    BUT I just ride my bike.

What do you do?

*Sing with actions
Sing the first verse of *My mother drives a tractor* putting actions to the words.

*Sing with props
Sing *My mother drives a tractor*, adding props such as a neckerchief, a chef's hat, a pilot's hat, a referee's whistle, a clown's wig, a rucksack, a football and a pretend bike! etc.

*Sing verses 2 and 3
Try singing the whole song, adding actions or props of your own.

**Who am I
Make a list of all the occupations that the group know. The leader then mimes the action of, e.g. a carpenter and says, "Who am I?" The first person to guess the correct answer "You are a ..." then takes over and so on.

**What jobs do the people in your family do?
"What jobs do the people in your family do?"
Reply: "My grandfather is a fishermanand my mother is a chemist."
Change leaders.

***Conversation 1
Voice 1: *"Good morning, (Naomi)."*
Voice 2: *"Good morning, (Oliver)."*
Voice 1: *"What does your father do?"*
Voice 2: *"My father is a teacher."*
Voice 1: *"My mother is a teacher too!"*
Voice 2: *"My mother is a baker."*

***Conversation 2
Voice 1: *"Hi (Sophie)."*
Voice 2: *"Hi (Sam)."*
Voice 1: *"What do you like to do?"*
Voice 2: *"I like to play (tennis)."*
Voice 1: *"Do any of your family play sport?"*
Voice 2: *"Yes, my (father) plays (tennis)."*
Voice 1: *"My (grandmother) plays (tennis) too, but she likes (golf) best."*

***Make up more
Divide the group into pairs and ask them to make up their own conversation (either about their favourite activities or about jobs) to perform to everyone else.

Can you tell me the time, please?

50–53
Capo: 1st fret

Is it one o'clock?

*Click the time

Say this rhyme with the clicks before before singing the song.

click	click
1 o'clock,	2 o'clock,
3 or 4 or	5 o'clock.
6 o'clock,	7 o'clock,
8 or 9 or	10 o'clock. It's
past,	eleven, *ssh!*
ssh! no	12, *ssh!*
ssh! o'	clock.

*Sing and tap

Sing *Can you tell me the time, please?* tapping a leg or foot in time (instead of clicking).

*Watch the clock

Using a clock to show the hours, the leader says, *"Can you tell me the time, please?"* Reply: *"It is (3 o'clock)."* And so on.

**Is it one o'clock?

The leader sets the clock to 3 o'clock and asks someone, *"Is it 1 o'clock?"* Reply: *"No, it's 3 o'clock?"* Change leaders.

**Draw a circle

Draw a circle, divide it in half and then in quarters. Write 'quarter past', 'half past' and 'quarter to'.

**Count in fives

Count in fives round the room until you reach 60.

**Add fives

Subdivide the quarters of your circle into threes. Starting from the top (both ways) add the figures 5, 10, 15, 20, 25, 30.

***What's the time, Mr Wolf?

Play this game outside. One person is chosen to be 'the wolf'. He walks away, followed by the others chanting:

All:　*"What's the time Mr Wolf?"*
Wolf: *"3 o'clock."*
All:　*"What's the time Mr Wolf?"*
Wolf: *"Half past 4"* and so on until,
All:　*"What's the time Mr Wolf?"*
Wolf: *"Time to eat you up!"*

***What time is this?

Using your clock, ask different times e.g.

5 past 4,	5 to 6
10 past 2,	10 to 5
20 past 11,	20 to 9
25 past 1,	25 to 7

***What time do you ...?

"What time do you wake up?"
Reply: *"I wake up at ..."*
"What time do you have breakfast?"
Reply: *"I have breakfast at ..."*
"What time do you go to school?"
Reply: *"I go to school at ..."*

What time is the bus for Liverpool?

54-56

What time is the bus for Li-ver-pool?— What time is the ve-ry last bus.——— What

time is the bus for Li-ver-pool?——— What time is the ve-ry last bus.———

Reply: It is ...

2. What time is the train for Nottingham?
What time is the very last train?
What time is the train for Nottingham?
What time is the very last train?
Reply: It is ...

3. What time is the plane for Paris?
What time is the very last plane?
What time is the plane for Paris?
What time is the very last plane?
Reply: It is ...

(left margin, top to bottom) 2.55 3.24 4.48 5.45 6.33 7.25 8.12 9.05 10.14 11.21 12.26

(top margin, left to right) 2.55 1.05 2.10 3.15 4.20 5.25 6.30 7.35 8.40 9.45 10.50 11.55 12.00 13.12 14.22 15.34

(right margin, top to bottom) 16.42 17.54 18.23 19.37 20.68 21.19 22.74 23.49 24.00

(bottom margin, left to right) 12.26 13.04 14.10 15.16 17.24 18.29 19.30 20.36 21.44 22.45 23.56 24.00

The bus departs at 22.15

*Sing and reply
Sing, *"What time is the very last bus?"* Reply: *"It is ..."* Change leaders.

*Say the reply
Sing all three verses together and repeat them until everyone has had a chance to say the reply.

*Add more
Add other place-names of towns and cities near you.

*Other transport
Add more verses including other forms of transport, e.g. *"What time is the boat ...?"*

**24-hour clock
Using a 24-hour clock, ask, *"What time is it?"* Reply: *"It is ..."* Change leaders.

**Make a list
Everyone writes down four things that they do in the day using the 24 hour clock, e.g. *"I get up at 7.30 I go to school at 8.30 I go home at 16. 00 I go to bed at 21.30"*

**Tell the time
Read out your list, e.g. *"I wake up at 7.15 I have breakfast at 8.00 I have lunch at 13.15 I have dinner at 19.30"*

**Make a daily timetable
Everyone makes a timetable of the things that they do at the same time daily, writing the times alongside. Use the 24-hour clock.

***Make a weekly timetable
Ask the group to the same, listing the important things that they do on a weekly basis.

***Conversation
Voice 1: *"Excuse me! What time is the ... for ...?"*
Voice 2: *"There is one every half hour. The next one is at ..."* or *"There is one in ... minutes."*
Voice 1: *"Where do I catch it from?"*
Voice 2: *"You catch it from ... station/airport."*
Voice 1: *"Thank you very much."*
Voice 2: *"Not at all."*
Voice 1: *"Goodbye!"*
Voice 2: *"Goodbye!"*

Goodbye, goodbye, goodbye

57-58*

Good - bye, good-bye, good - bye,_____ We have to say good - bye._____ We'll (I) (I'll)

see you soon on Mon - day, good - bye, good-bye, good - bye!_____

2. Tues - day
3. Wed - nes - day
4. Thurs - day
5. Fri - day
6. Sat - ur - day
7. Sun - day

* The recordings begin a 4th lower, in D major, and rise a semitone for each verse.
'Saturday' is therefore sung in G major (as notated here).

Thank you very much, goodbye everybody!   Spasibo bolshoye gospodi, gospoda. Dosvidanye!

33

Thank you very much, goodbye everybody!

*Listen and sing
Listen to one verse
of *Goodbye, goodbye,
goodbye*, then join in.

*I'll see you soon
Ask different people
to sing solo for *"I'll see
you soon on Monday"* etc.

*Sing in line
Form two lines facing
each other a few feet apart.
The top person of each line walks
towards the other while singing
"Goodbye, goodbye, goodbye" ;
they shake hands on *"we have to
say goodbye"* ; join hands and skip
down the middle of the two lines on
"we'll see you soon on Monday" and
walk backwards to join the bottom of
their respective lines on
"goodbye, goodbye, goodbye."
Begin again with a new top
couple, and so on.

**Sing in pairs
Ask everyone to join
hands with a partner and
swing round while singing
"Goodbye, goodbye, goodbye".
Face each other and clap
each others' hands, one
at a time, (twice) on
"we have to say goodbye" ;
slap knees and hands
(twice) on *"we'll see you
soon on Monday"* and then
swing round together on
"goodbye, goodbye, goodbye."

**Move on
Do the same as above
but this time on the last
"goodbye, goodbye, goodbye"
each person grabs a new
partner to dance with,
and the whole routine
begins again.

***Dance in fours
Form *sets* of four,
i.e. two couples facing
each other a few feet apart.
The four join hands and circle left
while singing *"Goodbye, goodbye,
goodbye"*. Two diagonal opposites
(*corners*) skip to the middle, link
arms, dance round and go back to
their places on *"we have to say
goodbye"* ; the other two do
the same on *"we'll see you
soon on Monday"*
(the two not dancing
clap in time), and then
all circle left again on
"goodbye, goodbye, goodbye."

***Goodbye,
around the world
Ask if anyone
knows the word for
'goodbye' in another language
as well as their own and
make a list of any new *'goodbyes'*.

Köszönöm viszontlàtàsra! Jerejef mangi dem! Merci beaucoup, au revoir messieurs-dames!

Danke sehr, meine Damen und Herren auf Wiedersehen!   Muchas gracias señores y señoras, adiós!

Molte grazie signori e signore, arrivederci! M-goy tsoy-geen! Ehfkhareesto ahndeeo!

How are you?　　What is this?　　Is this a ...?　　What day is it today?　　Have you got?

Is it Monday?　What's the date today?　When is your birthday?

How do you go to bed?　What time do you go to bed?　What time is the bus for ...?

34

Revision activities

Conversation for two

Rebecca: *"Good morning!"*
Michael: *"Good morning!*
Did you sleep well?"
Rebecca: *"Very well thank you."*
Michael: *"What would you like for*
breakfast?"
Rebecca: *"A croissant and some*
orange juice please."
Michael: *"Here you are."*
Rebecca: *"Thank you."*

What would you like to do today?

Hugh: *"What would you like to*
do today?"
Katy: *"I'd like to go to a (football)*
match."
Hugh: *"Do you like (football)?"*
Katy: *"Yes, I do. Do you?"*
Hugh: *"No, I prefer (rugby)."*
Katy: *"We could go to a (rugby)*
match if you prefer?"
Hugh: *"Let's go to (football) today*
and (rugby) next week."

When is your birthday?

Emma: *"When is your birthday?"*
Matthew: *"In (April)."*
Emma: *"What date in (April)?"*
Matthew: *"The (16th). When is*
yours?"
Emma: *"Mine is in (April too),*
(April 21st)."
Matthew: *"What would you like to do*
on your birthday?"
Emma: *"I'd like to go to (Paris)."*
Matthew: *"By train or by plane?"*
Emma: *"By train."*
Matthew: *"Let's go together."*

Put your hands up if you like ...?

Say *"Put your hands up if*
you like (cricket)" or *"Put your*
hands up if you don't like (cricket)."
Make a list to find out which is the
most popular – and the most
unpopular – sport among
your group.

My favourite games

Ask each of the group
to describe a favourite
party game that everyone
can play. Make a collection
of these games in one book,
including word games,
such as easy crosswords,
and card games. The book
would make a good birthday
or Christmas present.

Thank you very much, goodbye!

Adam: *"Excuse me! Can you tell*
me the time, please?"
Lucy: *"It is (22.15)."*
Adam: *"Where can I catch the*
bus for (Liverpool)?"
Lucy: *"From here."*
Adam: *" What time is the last*
bus?"
Lucy: *"It is at 22.45."*
Adam: *"Thank you very much,*
goodbye!"

Percussion ideas

timpani

Body percussion
Remember that actions are often body percussion and great fun to use before getting out the claves, maracas and tambourines.

Playing encourages singing
Children who do not enjoy singing will invariably prefer playing and can therefore be encouraged to join with the singing too. To start with, use percussion sparingly so that you can watch and check that the instruments are being used correctly.

Creative percussion
The best use of percussion will be the ideas that you and your group will come up with yourselves! There are some ideas below.

glockenspiel

snare drum

side drum

*Good morning, class
Use percussion instead of clicks. Claves are good as they give a good, clear sound. Use a repeated sound "Mis-ter Eng-lish" playing this on maracas or egg shakers all the way through the song. Try whispering "Mis-ter Eng-lish" with the whole group while listening to the CD to internalise the rhythm before using instruments.

*What would you like to do today?
Using an xylophone, chime bars or glockenspiel, find D and A. Play these as a steady beat together under the song.

**Can you tell me the time, please?
Create a tick tock sound with half the group being tick and other half tock. Start by saying tick tock together, then break up into two parts. After this add two instruments – encouraging everyone to recognise the difference between on-beat (tick) and off-beat (tock).

*** Have a happy, hippy, hoppy, happy birthday
Create a sound wall using an ostinato (repeated) rhythm for each line. Choose three types of instruments, one for each rhythm.
Part 1: Happy, hippy birthday
quick, quick, quick, quick, slow, slow
Part 2: Continuous beat to fit with Part 2.
Part 3: Happy birthday – same rhythm as the words in Part 3.

chime bars

hand chimes

bongos

tambor

bass drum

marimba

CD track list

The band:
Sam Swallow (Piano)
Ben Lumsden (Bass guitar)
Louisian Huba (Drums)